Lean Analytics

Manage and Automatize Your Business with Lean Analytics

(Data Analytics Made Easy)

Jason Bennett & Jennifer Bowen

Table of Contents

Introduction

Make the most of your production process, your tools, and workforce. Bring more cohesiveness to your relationship with success through the use of Lean Analytics. In this book, "Lean Analytics," you learn one of the foremost technologies used in the workplace. The focus is on aligning new directions in the thought process to improve work output.

Most management processes need constant supervision and overhauling. The Lean Analytic method handles the corrections on its own. Make short-term and long-term plans for business growth with the knowledge of the cost reductions and enhancement in the workplace productivity made possible by Lean Analytics.

Like, Business Intelligence tools use intelligent entities to integrate the work and management seamlessly reduces the stress on the workforce. And, machines that work without any sleep or wake notification to help watch critical systems and provide continuous feedback to improve the work output in a tremendous way.

Increased productivity in most cases implies a need for increased surveillance and governance. But, since you integrate the work process with the dynamic parameters of Lean, the Office Management becomes a snip. Analysis, Improvement, and Control naturally follow the Defining and Measurement of the parameters of production.

Through Lean, you keep the heartbeat of the process (*Takt*) in synchrony with the flow of the work. You can manage transition periods and waste generated without affecting the workflow. You need to become familiar with the Lean Manufacturing Tools and intertwine improvements through Lean practices.

Thereby, you reduce the time and increase the margin and profits to the organization. Reduced effort translates to reduced cost. Lean helps improve the customer satisfaction by always keeping the end in sight in its operations.

Consistent quality with improved control is the basis of the operating system. By improving the responsiveness of the business and getting rid of internal processes without any value, you achieve your aim of customer satisfaction and retention. Improving delivery parameters is integral in Lean.

Chapter 1 - Introduction to Lean Analytics

Lean is a creation by Toyota Business section of the Toyota Motor Company. It is aimed at improving the efficiency in the manufacturing process. All those who involved with the manufacturing process will have knowledge of the "lean" principles though this is not a needed condition.

Lean is a way of thinking applicable to the entire organization and not only the production process. And, Lean is not a cost-reduction process or a program that dictates a shortcut. The thought process defines what is lean in an organization and in the supply chain (*Lean Thinking*, By Womack and Dan Jones).

Founders of Lean

Jim Womack and Dan Jones are the founders of Lean Enterprise Academy. They also founded the Lean Enterprise Institute and the research team under their leadership coined the term "lean." But, many of the companies, such as the Toyota Production System chose not to use the term lean. They used their own definition for the term. But, in essence, the principles used remained the same.

From the time when Henry Ford lined up the steps in a production process in the 1900s, to the present day, the revolutionary assembly line caters to the demands of an ever-growing fabrication and processing industry.

While Ford's processing lines lacked the variety but had the finesse to provide a wide-ranging inventory, the more modern Toyota Production System shows how simple innovations to the original flow process can produce more continuity in the process flow.

Change Significant to Lean

So the focus shifted from the responsibility of the engineer committed to his machine, to the broad perspective of the movement of the product in relation to the entire process. They incorporated simple things like the use of the correct machine size for the volume of production needed and adding changes to the working of the machine to handle the small changes needed in the part number to maintain the output volume.

By sifting through these principles further, Womack and Jones reduced the number of principles to five. This is the 5S of Lean Analytics.

- Make a specific definition of the *value* needed by the customer.
- Give a shape for the *value stream* by understanding the value that would go into each product and get rid of all wasted steps.
- Align more steps with value to the existing ones so that the product has an enhanced *flow value*.
- If two steps remain separated, provide *pull* between them so that the flow value gets enhanced.

The accent is on reducing the time needed, the knowledge you will use, and the amount of effort you use (read number of steps) to achieve *perfection* in the service of the customer.

1. Value. Only the customer's need gives us value. You get value according to the timeline for production and delivery. The price point defines another sign of value. Did you meet any quality specifications? These define the value in the product and service we provide. You have the most demand in the market when you are the only manufacturer that can provide the value the customer seeks.

2. Value stream. After we have defined the value in full, we sum it up to get the value stream. This accounts for the entire raw material we take and the entirety of the products we make and relates it to the processes. The processes included will have administration, procurement, design, HR, production, customer service, and delivery. Right from the physical activity involved in the production and management of services, to solving problems, and managing information needed for the implementation of the workforce, Lean Analytics help categorize waste so you may cut them out. Here the underlying steps involve three kinds of steps – value-adding steps, value-enabling (does not add value but the process needs them), and non-value processes.

3. Flow. When we bring the processes to one page, we can find and get rid of those that do not add value to the product. This number crunching becomes possible due to the bird's eye view we have on the processes, material, products, and services. Identify the interruptions, delays, and bottlenecks – anything that proves detrimental to the value of the product and remove them. Here we enhance the flow by tightening the circle of steps that links the value and have value. You stop thinking in a vertical way and extend techniques and possibilities across all departments. This type of cross-functional working method helps ease the strain and improve cohesiveness in the approach to delivering key customer values. This approach helps improve productivity and efficiency by 40-45% in specific areas. The continuum in productivity, information, and services helps do away with upstream buildup until the downstream demand comes through.

4. Pull. In any normal ERP type of production, one makes the products as per the forecast of the demand and the need of the

schedule. In the Pull system, there is no production until the customer orders the product. To achieve this productivity rate, you need very small productivity cycles including those of the design and the delivery of the product. It has an inbuilt information cycle that keeps the downstream informed of its activities on that day.

5. Perfection. To achieve product perfection, total quality management undergoes continuous and systematic overhauling. This key attitude symbolizes the unyielding pursuit of perfection through the removal of unneeded process and methods.

Today, we have many hundreds of books written on the subject due to the continued success of Lean. This remains reflected by the rising market shares and sales in those enterprises using Lean technology.

We use it in almost all spheres of life including healthcare services, logistics, and routine maintenance. You can find it in government institutions, construction activities, and retail industry.

Perfection is the aim and we create this when we get a perfect value without any waste. Spreading the infectious attitude of Lean to the customers and other firms in the supply and distribution chain remains a wonderful by-product of Lean.

By optimizing the technologies used, and realigning the focus of the management, each product and service reaches or passes through its perfect value in the demand curve. And remember one of the golden rules of Lean, "Slow Processes are Expensive."

Chapter 2 - Lean Analytics to Succeed

Set the Flow Path

Implementing the Lean Analytics envisages the use of change in the thinking at the workplace. The first step to achieve this is to make a pivotal point in the hierarchy. When we use this, the clarity in the workplace remains enhanced. In most normal cases, this occurs by implementing the agent for change. This person remains responsible for all changes brought into force through Lean.

By choosing one leader, it becomes possible to revert any changes that do not work. This happens by streamlining the work through this central point. Also, we make the responsible person take action for all the work-related activity.

So, if there is no action from the responsible person, the downstream activity ceases. Only when the leader agrees and approves of the changes, the rest of the work undergoes implementation.

The work then proceeds forward and the same condition gets applied to further activity. The change remains regulated by streamlining it through the central point of activity. And when any change gets detected that is not normal or expected, all the further downstream activity ceases.

Once this flow path has come into force, it is easy to govern the natural evolutionary process for downstream activity.

Use the Services of a Lean Consultant

Learning the Lean Path is essential. It is easy to govern the workers once the process has begun. But, only the people who are conversant with the method of Lean will know when to make the needed changes.

The knowledge is needed for the parallel working types in Lean that control each other. All the decisions and management principles remain data-driven and systemized through actual use.

For instance, you have two or three HR situations, which do not yield, direct answers in a normal analysis. One is the case where the turnover is low and the number of employees leaving the firm is rising. Next, the budget for training is big, but there is no clear-cut region where employee deployment will be profitable. And third, the hiring expense rises all the time due to attrition among the employees at the workplace.

To arrive at the solution, get a snapshot of the metrics. This will give a view of the nature of the problem. Check the metrics in related areas and see if there is any correlation. Use of KPI gives you the answers needed to make the changes.

You can make use of pre-designed KPI software to do the analysis. It helps you to centralize the data related to the business and simplify real-time reporting. Actionable work gets broken into smaller pieces and removed until only those relevant to the work remain.

Use a Lever to Begin the Transformation

Most of the hardships one faces are situations begging for alternatives. And, every business undergoes these situations often. Rather than wait for a crisis to begin to make the change, begin the movement towards Lean by initiating the change yourself.

When you face a troublesome situation, one must change. The Lean philosophy anticipates changes and makes provisions for each. By preparing for the change, it is possible to overcome the negativity and create the positivity that will take the business to a profitable end.

This situation applies to the client, the business owner, and the suppliers involved in transacting business.

The other alternative is to change the focus so that the problem does not seem as large. The Lean expert waits until the crisis has passed before he seeks the solution. In doing so, he gets a solution with ease.

Do Not Aim for Grand Solutions

The idea is avoidance of the key issues that precipitate the issue and look for solutions away from the hotspot. Many business problems solve themselves if you give it enough time. With this in mind, the Lean expert tries to figure out how to keep the mechanism of the business moving without overlapping in the key problem areas.

The first thing to do is to stop thinking of grand solutions. You will not get anything that will heal the situation instantly. And if you continue to think along those lines, you will only become disillusioned. It is better to think of small actionable solutions that have a better chance of working.

If you consider applying growth metrics in the workplace, you need to apply the Lean Analytics related to this metric. This includes the acquisition to growth employee life cycle and the lifecycle during retention. You must then consider the cycle after attrition to reacquisition.

One may improve the bottom line impact in the HR department by using better resource application. Also, use cross-training across all departments. Using Lean, you can improve the sensitivity of the training program by a huge amount.

Make a Map with the Implementation Timetable

The scientific approach to the problem of making the map involves the use of the positivist perspective on one hand. And, you use the hermeneutic perspective on the other. In the first, the user remains distanced from the aim and the research problem.

The problem gets divided into smaller pieces so that there is the possibility of refining the process and cutting out the waste. In the second method, the researcher remains central to the problem. All the flow processes get importance relative to him and those processes that lose their importance get eliminated.

The creation of the timetable helps to improve the flow value and the perspective. Each work function becomes more important or less important because they have to meet the time check.

When the tasks fail to meet the time check, we check for alternative solutions that have a better possibility of meeting the timetable.

Take the First Step Immediately

It is important for progress in any business to begin activity immediately. This means that one uses any one of the scientific approaches existing between theory and reality to come through with an action plan.

In the most normal case, one uses the induction-deduction method. These are opposing methods of analysis and find applicability to any kind of work situation.

If you have the reality worked out, then there is no need for any deep analysis. One may put into action the plan in a step by step approach. Inductive reasoning finds a use for most of the cases where there are no real results and the opinion remains needed to take the next step.

In the deductive or scientific method, there is an existing theory. This means that the reality is apparent. So, you can use it to proceed to the next step. The main focus is to show visible activity.

This will set off the process and the chain reaction will continue until there is no more productivity. To see the result, one must begin the first step immediately.

Check for the Results Immediately

It is important to check the results fast and see the amount of progress one has made. Changes to the amount of working capital show in a clear way to all. But, the deeper metrics such as the Return on Equity and Vendor Expenses may not come to light as fast. Yet, these will impact the business in a big way.

If you know what you owe your vendors now and what you have owed them in the past, it will help you to optimize the expenses and streamline production. You need to set the benchmarks and targets for the vendors in the first place.

By checking the results immediately, you will know if you made the right decision and if so, how much profit is accruing from this.

You make use of Lean thinking and methods to improve profitability through timely action. You also cut the redundant processes. By concentrating on the processes that have more value, you improve the efficiency and lower the labor overheads.

Use Progressive Results into Value Stream Building

One side of the Lean method is where one cuts the unneeded processes. The other side is where one builds the processes that show positive results. When implementing qualitative processes, there is a lesser amount of control.

You can improve the formalization and grade of control by the use of quantitative structures.

Use of real-time targets will cut the amount of uncertainty and bring more cohesiveness into play. For the practical values, one must use tests and questions. Then, one must study documents and information registers before using the suggested values.

But, once you do this, you have a viable working system that you can depend on.

Chapter 3 - The Metrics That Matters For Your Business

Learning to use Lean resources and principles is half the battle. Also, you will come across questions such as, "Is Lean better than Six Sigma?" Or, "Is it better to use the Theory of Constraints?" When you use more than one method, you will get lost. One may get over the arguments over philosophical or even technical differences with ease. You only have to stick to the basic Lean principle of *avoiding excess and getting rid of waste.*

Overview of Over-Production

The production cycle has in-built questions to start the next cycle. The first one is to please only the customer and stop when you reach the target. Have I achieved today's quota? If the answer is yes, then stop production. Until the customer places a new order, do not make anything.

This principle applies to all departments in the organization. The idea is to achieve the perfect value stream. Other than this, there is nothing you need to worry about. In Lean, we reduce the steps we use to help cut waste, while the Six Sigma principle checks for variation.

The more variations there are in the process, the more chances there are for waste to accumulate. You need to follow only Lean principles of keeping the number of steps down.

Use of Lean Principle at Work

To separate technicality from the working, it is important the workers understand and use Lean principles. Often, there are problems that seem technical in nature but involve real people.

You begin to use Lean principle at the core, the place where the problem arises with only one man. Then, expand the core team to as many as you need, until the problem gets resolved.

It takes some time for the principles to go into operation because there is a learning curve involved. If you do not have the Lean thinking, then there will not be much progress.

Also, the team must know if the circumstances are right. If they are not, they must identify the cause and size of the problem. It may be due to one or more of the following:

1. Lack of commitment: The worker does not feel there is a need for Lean methods. He uses traditional principles but gets foxed when others seem to feel something is extraneous. Shift the focus and reexamine the problem.

2. Performance not aligned with commitment: This is more serious because work is ongoing and the value is not reaching the expected level. We need a change in the attitude because the worker wants to get measured according to the performance parameter. He is not worried about the process parameter.

3. Lack of training: The workers get deployed before they have got trained. So, they keep looking at the others when the work proceeds. Change the worker to another place and keep the work going. Wait until the person addresses the problem by confronting it.

We see that the Lean working method is not a toolbox we can pick from to achieve our ends. It is a total perspective that involves the entirety of the work process.

When you see a segmentation of the workforce, say the people on the shop floor working at a different pace from the rest of the workers, you face a problem. Here the plant manager has to hit the stop button. Slow down the process, check where overproduction occurs.

He has a target to meet and must keep the workforce occupied. But, he can do other work and still meet the target. This is the Lean principle. Any extraneous work gets eliminated first. By moving the focus of the work to a new place, any kind of waste, in material or labor, is got rid of.

The people need to have a Lean eye to develop the perspective they can depend on. This helps them understand how the factory works with each component getting linked to the next. They learn to recognize the elements that are important and work with these first.

Choose to Operate the Pull

You have many aspects affecting how to operate the Pull. The Pull is important because there will be instances where the workflow gets interrupted. One of the ways to use it is to address the question or problem from two or more perspectives.

Pull exists at the nodes or joints of the structure in the organization. The workflow question is, "Have you finished this work?" The problem question is, "Where is the box of material I am supposed to deliver?" And the Pull question becomes, "Who is the driver delivering the box to the work spot?" You can change the Pull in many ways until you have got rid of the externality existing in the structure.

So, you see the work proceeding, but there is a lag due to the lack of the box. The Lean principle tells you to cut the waste. Here you are wasting time. To cut this, you must address the issue by finding out who is bringing the box.

The truck needed to deliver the box must undergo preparation. And then the box must get loaded onto the truck. But, since there is a problem, you shift the focus of the problem by diverting the loaders to a new place to do new work.

The problem is now resolved at two or three levels. One is the basic worker level where you give new work to the worker. The second is at the management level where you identify what caused the lack of the box.

The third is at the deployment level where you keep alternatives ready to prevent any further occurrence of this event. Lean, thus, operates at many levels.

Make Comparison of the Steps

As the value stream progresses, the number of options keep on adding up. Many businesses keep these options open in the hope that some good will come of it. But, it ends up as a waste of space and effort.

So, it is wise to get rid of all but one working option. When you have more than one option, it will end up in confusion.

If you have to make a choice, list out the options. Then, compare the merits and demerits of each one.

Try reducing the steps in each and see, which one gets done first. This will prove to be the best choice.

Chapter 4 - Key Metrics and Your Own Targets

Have the best working stream by working upward from the fundamentals. This involves the integration of the organizational structure and deployment of the tools needed to work. The value stream management focuses on improving shared vision and helping workers achieve their goal.

Lean Thinking helps Business Systems to Grow

Systems and processes remain based on principles. Here we use the 5S principles of Lean thinking to build our business model. The idea behind developing the business system is to plan and create a strategy.

We also use it for development and implementation of the business process. You meet customer expectation and add value to the brand.

For this, you have to measure, compare, and analyze the customer based parameters. The Lean thinking points out the areas to develop and those you can eradicate. When you create more space, you see the demand grow among the customers. They seek newer things and want them faster.

The business system helps you meet this demand and by using Lean, you can get the best value for the customer.

You have good employee engagement and due to the business system, you have consistent results. It helps you make a profit by reducing the labor needed and improving the time factor.

Use policy deployment

The purpose of initiating a working policy or strategy is to expose the customer to the goals of the origination. It translates the vision and strategy into Key Performance Indicators by setting targets.

You can also deploy change projects at various levels in the organization. Strategy deployment plays a crucial role in determining the alignment of the working method. This helps the management in four crucial ways.

1. It improves the delivery factor by prioritizing where to deploy targets.
2. There is a clear link established between the Lean approach and the business outcome.
3. The senior management team gets clarity of purpose.
4. You see the engagement of the employees according to the priorities.

Make an Accounting System Based on Lean

Compared to traditional business methods the Lean Accounting System remains based on financial performances. It also considers non-financial attributes such as timeliness, efficiency, quality, and so on. The traditional systems placed their focus on overhead absorption and labor efficiency.

Continuous improvement remains the main target of the Lean accounting system with Value Stream Process being central to everything. The effort is to increase the flow through suitable Lean strategies. Employees get motivated and empowered to use the Lean thinking so there is the change present throughout the organization.

Due to the improved flow, we find increased accountability and quicker turnaround. This comes under the control of the Value Stream Team

Management that takes into account the entire value streams and not any individual ones.

Calculation of costs encompasses three broad groups. One is the raw materials and input costs. The next includes the conversion and processing costs. And the last one covers the facility cost.

Change the Pay to Reflect the Lean Thinking

The first thing to do is to improve the focus on things that add value. The process comes to nothing if it makes something that the customer does not want. But, there will always be some element of the process that does not add value to the system. Identify the people who add value and reward them.

This will encourage them to work better. The process will become more efficient and the customer will have more satisfaction.

Another way to do this is to make bonus payments on occasions or if we have increased productivity. This is the way the management gives thanks to the employees for their dedication to the work. In the same way, remove any work that does not add value to the customer. You will cut loss through this Lean method.

When you invest in the Lean Analytics, you get profit whenever there is a redundancy in the process.

You also get profit due to the increased efficiency of the people in the organization. To keep the output high, you must pay the people having higher efficiency.

Define Performance Measurement Well

To improve participation and for better deployment of tools related to Lean, the team must make sure that everyone understands what the performance-defining parameters are.

For instance, if you want better employee attendance, tell the workers how they will get the bonus points if they are present ahead of time. When the employee knows what is going to reward him, he will keep looking for that. This is the basis of Lean thinking.

By choosing the suitable indicators, you can increase or decrease the rate of production, improve the quality of the output, and inspire better performances from the workforce.

Once the employees begin to appreciate the Lean thinking, they will adopt it and you will have less loss due to inefficiency at work.

Studying the metrics of what you do is a very important part of having a successful business. Without looking at the numbers you really cannot know exactly why you experienced either success or failure.

You can make assumptions, but when you don't have to do that it is better to use facts to ensure that your efforts are not a waste.

Indeed analytics can tell you what happened, why it happened, what will happen and how you can make it happen.

If you want to grow your business and plan exactly where it is going, use analytics to discover insights into your business that will help you accomplish that goal.

More Training for All Employees

One way to increase employee participation is to keep changing the way you instruct them.

They have a method of understanding things and once you hit the right method of speaking or instructing them, they will understand and work faster and better. The other way is to give training to all employees so they are able to work well.

This can be in the form of workshops or even on-the-job training by employing a few supervisors who go around showing how to do things.

This is the best way to remove disinterest and low work productivity.

Make Use of Proper Tools for the Job

Use of wrong tools or tools of the wrong size will decrease productivity. Make checks to ensure that at all places in the workflow the tools are of the needed size.

You can improve work performance through the use of automated tools. This will reduce worker fatigue and also the time taken to do the work.

Chapter 5 - Data-Driven Approaches

To understand the bottlenecks in a workflow environment, we gather all the data affecting the flow. We feed this into the computer and use advanced Lean Analytics to understand the nature of the problem and get the possible solutions. Use of data helps to uncover hidden facts that a manual inspection might overlook. This is the primary motivation behind using the data-driven analytics.

The second thing is the change and the amount of change that the system will take for best functioning. Changing the value of the parameter one way might improve the profitability of the business.

But, it might prove detrimental to the other aspects affecting the flow. We use data analytics to understand the impact of the changes and how we can govern the individual aspects to suit the working of the business.

Improvement in the work must arise from the betterment of the individual. This is the basis of the Lean approach.

It transforms the thinking to such an extent that the thoughts of money and gain will vanish before that of adherence to quality and addition of values. So, where does one draw the line?

This is the vital question that the lean expert faces when he tries to use the data-driven approach at the workplace.

Building the Framework for the Lean Transformation

You have many readymade models to use to build your framework. These evolved over the years through continuous use and change and so they have a good degree of consistency and dependability built into them.

You can build your own framework by addressing the issues that you want to solve through the framework.

1. Which is the issue that affects us in a big way?
2. What is the basic structure of the culture at present? Do we drive it or change it?
3. What is the type of change we bring to the actual work?
4. Does the new way of working need any changes in the management systems? Do we need changes in the behavior of the leadership?
5. What method do we use to improve capability?

These questions apply to the framework at the micro and macro levels. The individual responsibility changes at each level depending on the framework size.

The system must address all related questions including ones that deal with interrelationships among the issues. If it does not, the transformation may lose its momentum.

Addressing the issues

First, address the issue that you face. This might be getting established in the local market, finding a good place for the business, or choosing a good name. Create hypothetical solutions and apply Lean methods to drop the inefficient ones.

Often, this is the starting point of the business and so you will need to address this and solve it completely.

If you are not satisfied with your present place or you do not have a place to operate from, then you must check the locality for another place. You can rent out an existing place or share space with an existing business.

If you want suggestions for the name, you can check the internet. There are many sites that give you suggestions for names.

Structure of the existing culture

This remains based on the place where you are. If you are a local person, then you will not have any problems fitting in. The method of movement and distribution of goods depends on the practices of the place. If you are not familiar with these, then you will not find many customers here.

The process of the implementation is simple. The user gathers the metrics to use with the site. Usually, the pattern of usage will change for each different user. You can add features to the website to improve usability or conversion.

So, a framework gets made. User testing feedback will give an idea of how well the site works and what improvements you need.

We analyze the work detail information for one kind of user. Lean programming helps us choose the right parameters for the use of the system. The performance gets tested and if this has a positive response, the number of users gets increased.

When the performance is satisfactory, the other users get included in the testing. The testing carries on until there is a uniformly positive response from the user.

Chapter 6 - Your Secret Weapon: KPI and Team Meetings

Growth comes from personal interaction with your team members at work. It does not matter whether you are the boss or the employee, if you are not communicating with your colleagues at the workplace, the office becomes a quagmire of confusion.

You will not relish going there. So, you will not get much work done either.

Integrating KPIs into the work stream helps you keep up with the changes and make progress along with them. The KPI is a Key Performance Indicator. It is a measurable aspect of the work that tells you whether you remain headed in the right direction or you need to change.

Choosing the right KPI is essential for correct performance estimation. These KPIs help to establish the operational and strategic goals of the company.

Organize the Value Stream according to the Product Groups

In the first part, you segregate the KPIs to improve the value flow. When you align the value stream, you set the protocol and ground rules along with it. Here you make a list of the attainable and relevant goals and set a time limit for it.

The products remain arranged according to the usage at various points of the workflow.

You must find the KPI for each of the product groups and estimate the best way to enhance the value. The advantage of using the KPI is that you can automate processes that previously needed the use of spreadsheets.

You can optimize productivity and decrease the decision-making time needed by the use of KPI for that product in the value stream.

Most of these indicators are standards specific to the industry where they find a use. The KPI helps you measure goals you make to reach your business aim. Here are some KPIs for different sectors.

1. Marketing – Site traffic, time of visitor on site, newsletter subscribers, and so on.
2. Sales – Margin, sales through existing customers, annual sales, and so on.
3. Banking – Customer retention, asset quality, customer base, and so on.

Trace the path of each product and service from start to finish in the production cycle. As given above, check the KPI and find the ones that matter. It will help you to group the KPIs according to their nature.

1. Qualitative
2. Quantitative
3. Directional
4. Practical
5. Actionable

Qualitative KPI reflects the level of attainment of the business aim. A positive value shows that you are achieving success. If you do not get this, you must work to develop the KPI toward the positive value. The

Quantitative KPI remains represented as numbers. This gives a more accurate source of information.

Directional KPI will show which way you and your business go at present. This is mostly used in the initial stages where you set up the business and do not have any other clear indicators of the growth.

Practical KPI is the one that shows your real-time position. This does not involve any calculations or predictions. And, the last is the actionable KPI that helps you make the changes you need for the business development.

Importance of Team Meetings

When you have the meetings, you have the team. The team that takes part in meetings knows what each of the others in the team does. They realize their responsibility and will chip in when it matters.

Make sure you have regular team meetings. The meetings must occur at least once a week and preferably once daily. The more interaction you have with the team, the stronger is the bond you develop and so you will contribute more value to the product.

The team meetings help the team members ask others about strategy and clarify doubts. This helps build camaraderie and trust.

Use the team meetings as the fulcrum for your business activities. It may involve interaction with the supply or distribution chain members. Or, it may have the board members meeting to discuss the strategy of the day.

Whatever it is, you are sure of one thing. It helps you know how the company stands and what your position is in the whole shebang. This system helps you establish the rhythm needed to promote your business well.

Setting up a Lean Promotion

The Lean technology uses the 5Ps to make the ideal Lean model. It deals with using focused energy to improve profit and efficiency. The first is the Purpose. The aim for which they make the project is the Purpose.

This may not always be money but could be one of the motives for the formation of the company. It may also have a philanthropic motivation.

The second P is the process that goes into the manufacture of the product or service. It details the internal working and the interface of interaction with its clients or customers.

The way they operate determines its success and its profile on the market. One of the most important P's is the People. It refers to the people who link with the product, the company, and the usage of its services. It shows the spectrum of people affected by the services or product.

The next P is the Platform. This is where they carry the product. It refers to the collection of tools and technologies that the company uses for its product. The platform may also mean the software or computer networks that the company uses to support its product.

The last P refers to the Performance. It shows how the company fulfills its obligation to its customer.

Manage the Personnel and Growth in the Company

If you use Lean standards, you will know that when you recruit people, you must watch against over-staffing. This does not mean that you recruit a lesser number of people than needed. You do not recruit people until there is a need for it. Instead of hiring and firing people, use the right number of people from the start.

Use the proper metrics for monitoring and promoting growth in the company on a short and long-term basis. It means that you align the resources, working process, and policy in a way that shows the increase in the performance and profits of the company.

It is the outlook you maintain for the future to help use plans that help improve the position of the company in the market. Lean helps you by optimizing the steps you use for this purpose.

Chapter 7 - Automatize the Company Thanks to the Analytics

Lean Analytics help you track the metrics vital to the growth and profitability of your business. The first step involves identifying those that are good. So, what is a good metric? A good metric is one that satisfies the following criteria:

- **You can understand a good metric**

This is important because unless people understand the metric and discuss it, they will not try to get involved. Only when people are involved in the change, the metric has a real impact on the growth of the company.

- **It is comparable**

The users and people in your company can relate to the change of the metric over time. They remember the time when the metric was not growing so fast or when the growth slowed almost to a standstill. They discuss this aspect with the metric of a different company or competitor. It makes them involved in the growth process.

- **Ratios and rates are good metrics**

The nature of ratios and rates make them good metrics. This is because they already relate to something and so you get the growth aspect straight by reading the number given. If you have this kind of metrics, use them as they will help you develop the true picture of the company and its growth.

- **Metrics are adaptable**

The changes you have in the business remain reflected by the metric. First, you must be able to read the metric. Then, you must be able to use the metric. An adaptable metric is more useful than one that is not.

Find the stage your business is in

You know what business you deal with and so you can arrive at the metrics involved in the process. To find the stage you are at, check the gating metrics.

- Empathy
- Stickiness
- Virality
- Revenue
- Scale

Starting from the lowest one, you can pass onto the next gate by checking your present position. For instance, if you have found a need in the market that did not have enough suppliers, then you pass through the Empathy Gate.

At the second stage, you find the MVP (Minimum Viable Product) that satisfies the customers in the market now. The MVP has only the bare minimum features but takes care of the need of the customers. This is the Stickiness stage and the early users will find your solution easy to use.

The third analytic stage is Virality. It means that you have the product with all the features that the customer looks for and they like it. You need to make your product more cost efficient and attainable. Once you do this, you can pass on to the next stage. This stage is the Revenue stage where you get involved in the economics of the product. Find means to optimize the revenue.

The calculation involves determining how much of money you expect from the customer and how much money you spend to get the customer. If the first amount is at least three times the second, you have good margins. This brings you to your last stage. This we call Scale.

The Scale is the stage where you grow your business. You can make plans to allow the business to grow. More than getting the metrics and working with it, you should make the wise choice of metrics at all times. This means that you should work with one metric that matters to you most. This may be Churn.

If the Churn is less than 3%, it means your business is stable and growing. But, if the Churn is more than 3%, then it means that your business is in trouble and that you have to take action.

Use Metrics for Your Automation

Automation means letting the machines, here computers, do the work. This will involve three big steps other than the calculation and the setting up of metrics. They are as described below:

Put a Global Strategy based on Lean into Place

To be a global player, the businessman must have the access to the foreign markets. It is easy to build the market through the supply chain network or the sub-network if you invest enough money. This step is crucial and once this is in place, you have the means to merge your gains through Lean.

Every market has its risks and international exposure brings its own share with it. Use Lean methods of testing and placing new footholds in the market. Eliminating wasteful methods and time-consuming processes will be the starting point in the process.

Many companies used low-risk and low-cost strategies for making the market entry. One example of this is export. This proved fruitful for those companies that did not face much competition. Using the Lean strategy of labor reduction and cost optimization proved beneficial to the businessmen.

- Use of mobile app monetization
- Applicability of media sites
- Balance the inventory
- Create website content

You can hire the local delivery services to take care of making deliveries in foreign lands. This is the first basis for expansion. The second is to establish an online presence that helps you become a household name.

You need to use mobile-friendly content and ads. This will get you to most of the people in the world because they all use mobile phones.

Completing the Transformation

Create an SEO friendly website that has links to heritage sites. Only this helps you establish your product on the internet. Facebook, Twitter, Tumblr, Instagram, WhatsApp, and the others provide more exposure for your product. Provide the links for all these on your website.

Conduct contests that give rewards to the users that link your website to the most number of sites. The publicity is cheap but effective.

Get your customers and suppliers into the Lean chain

Integrating the supply chain and the delivery network through the market and finding the best point of entry and delivery for your product is the first step. Value stream management has lots of interest among Lean users because of the way it gives the best solution. To maintain market viability, you need to have a good delivery system.

The supply chain will succeed if your end users remain satisfied. Value-adding activities for your product will depend on the choice and deployment of the decoupling points.

While agile systems are best applied to the downstream side of the decoupling point, the Lean system gets applied to the upstream side.

Use good bookkeeping software to keep track of the inventory and bill management. Also, add good content to your website to attract more visitors.

Use well-written content by a professional to add real value to the website.

Conclusion

In this book, "Lean Analytics," you learned how to use Lean technology. The success of Lean technology remains epitomized by the Toyota Motor Company that is on its way to becoming the largest automaker in the world.

Application of Lean Analytics helps you explore possibilities in every sphere and at all levels within an organization. You can use Lean in your workplace and if you have difficulty, use the services of a Lean expert.

Lean improves workplace efficiency by changing our approach to problems and in the way we figure out the solution. It is growing due to its continued success and will remain one of the dominant technologies of the future.

References

https://www.lean.org/LeanPost/Posting.cfm?LeanPostId=135

https://productcoalition.com/agile-and-lean-practices-for-data-driven-product-development-abb917b4e1e3

https://dev.to/topriddy/data-driven-developmentlean-programming

https://www.leanmethods.com/resources/articles/what-business-system-and-why-do-you-need-one/

https://www.educba.com/lean-analytics/

www.ingramcontent.com/pod-product-compliance
Lightning Source LLC
Chambersburg PA
CBHW071151220526
45468CB00003B/1016